Copyright © 2015
By Ἐπὶ Σχεδίας Publications & Leonidas Galazis
All rights reserved.

This book or any portion thereof may not be reproduced or used in any manner whatsoever without the express written permission of the publisher except for the use of brief quotations in a book review or scholarly journal.
First Printing: 2013, in Greek, entitled *Dokimes Synkolliseos*.

ISBN: 978-9963-2158-0-5

Translation: Georgia Galazi - Edited by Despina Pirketti
Cover: "Apollo in the Forge of Vulcan", by Diego Velázquez, 1630

Ordering Information:
info@episxedias.com, lgalazis@gmail.com

Trials on Welding

BY THE SAME AUTHOR

POETRY

Bloody Corals (Matomena Corallia), Lefkosia, 1979.
The Pest and Other Poems (O loimos kai alla poiimata), Lefkosia, 1981.
Medical Certificate (Iatriki Vevaiosi), Lefkosia, 1982 (State Prize for New Writer)
Acrid Quinces (Styfa kidonia), Lefkosia, 1988.
Fotilasia, Lefkosia, 1999.
Floundering in Alphabet (Paradarmos en Alphabito), Lefkosia, Chr. Andreou Editions, 2007.
Lokrigana, Athens, Gabriilides Editions, 2010 (National Poetry Prize).
Trials On Welding (Dokimes Synkolliseos), Athens, Farfoulas Editions, 2013.

ESSAYS

Personification in Costas Montis Poetry (I prosopopoiisi sto poiitiko ergo tou Costa Monti), Athens, Gabriilides Editions, 2008.
Poetics and Ideology in Cyprus Theatre (1869-1925) (Poiitiki kai ideologia sto kypriako theatro 1869-1925) (Ph. D. Thesis), Lefkosia, Cultural Services, Ministry of Education and Culture, 2012.
Textual Refractions (Keimenikes diathlaseis), Athens, Iolkos Editions, 2012.

Trials on Welding

Leonidas Galazis

Translated by Georgia Galazi
Edited by Despina Pirketti

In memory of my father

ALONG THE PATH OF AGIASMATA

Barefoot in patched clothes
you were scurrying down the paths
of the cloistered Agiasmata.
Red grapes
to the archangels flanking you.

Defenceless shadows around
your relic.

Your mother on the mountain crest
flag glimmering
"in the matudinal hours"
as when you were a child
holding the hexapteryga.

Red grapes –
alone in the vineyards of Ano Madari.

Alone, all alone.

Black olives and stale bread
though the rodents be grinding their teeth;
vinegar and gall
you were given to drink
by those now looking
at dust on their clothes.

Alone!

And your father bent over the anvil
casting to fire the terrible secrets.

THE GLARES REMAIN

"... the sparks [...] reached high as the sky, they became stars."

— Argyris Chionis, *"Esotika topia"*

Don't look, you said, with the naked eye
at the blinding glares of my welding.
But I would often trick you
to determine with my own eyes the extent of the damage.
Other than that I would obey
though often bothering you with frequent questions.
For instance, I didn't know why every now and then
you banged against the hot metal with the sledgehammer
nor could I understand at the time
why you had me thoroughly remove the rust
from the surface of the metal
with a hard brush and rasps.
Though now I do understand that the germ of rust
they carry in their composition
and bring it with them.

At least the glares remain
and the elusive frolics of the sparks
which in a split second cool down
and collapse immediately
on the floor heavy-hearted like humble grindings of iron.

VIGILANT SPARKS

"...but it always was, and is, and shall be, an ever living fire, kindled in due measure, and in due measure extinguished."

— Heraclitus

A few sparks were vigilant though
under the dead grindings
and when least expected
a point of origin onto the floor
(staying there, vigilant!)
and all the grindings were ascending again
as they sang
dancing like crazy in the air
before falling back on the floor
and I thought they were already dead
but you, father, were fully aware
of the dilatory tactics of the grindings
never quitting
carefully taking cover instead
under successive layers of ash
and when least expected they become alive
(staying there, alive)
and they stir the depths of our soul
dancing frantically inside the furnace of our soul.

Staying there forever alive
on the floor
and you are looking at them
unwearyingly
unconcerned
about the flammable materials close by!

DEPARTURE

What a fright your cat took
when the two strangely adorned strangers
walked into the house uninvited!
And how it nearly jumped out of its skin,
poor cat, as it faced their dog
their pale horse, swords and hawk!

It hid in a corner of the yard and waited
not foreseeing
that in a few minutes the neighbours would show up
and the ambulance, pale;
that your children wouldn't make it on time.

The cat – to this day refusing to believe
that you are forever gone.

Who will tend it now
by whose feet will it sit
who will it playfully ask for caresses
to whose words will it hearken?

THE COINS

"Smiling with one eye, tears in the other;
the tear shows her grief, the laugh her deceit."

— Bergades, "*Apokopos*":267-268

The ravens came dressed
for the occasion.

Evil tongues
of tropical storms.

Upon their slim body stolen glances
burying the coins of betrayal.

And they kept digging out awls,
threads and spools
miserable masks
to hide their envious laughter
lest it would betray them.

You were there, watching them
behind the vigil lamp in sorrow.

STERILE SENTIMENTS

The scalpel of memory.
There were stains on the floor
and the horse with the perforated wings.

Parchments in the corridors drops of lemon
and sin-washing
in secret basins
where they great take care
to imbue memories
with the potent liquids of oblivion
until you can't even remember your name.

Pills, injections, bindweed dressed-in-white Samaritans
with sterile sentiments.

And we, head bowed, were looking at those birds
shearing away.
And raindrops
were chasing us without mercy.
Venom!

THE DUST

They were looking at the dust
on their clothes
not at the earth
that covered you forever.

At the dust on their clothes
they were looking for the first time
as if the rain
could forget
the syringes
draining your bone marrow
as the son of the Night
lurked
in the annotations
of voluminous medical prescriptions.

ROWING AWAY ON YOUR OWN

For three days your mother locked
the unruly goats inside the pen...

How could she ever imagine
the pathways of medical protocols
at the sight of which even her fearless goats
would run away in fright?

How could she have locked
the sallow horse
inside the pen for days on end
when all the dead would rise from sleep
their bitterness to dampen
each corner of the world?

And if by chance she did lock it,
in what yards would
the awful horseman wander about
in spite of his mother's biddings?

Rowing away now, all on your own!

Where did the boatman go?

The rusty piastres
thickened black water
and the dreadful fumes
of the souls.

ANO MADARI

On the foothills of Ano Madari
carrying your soul on a platter
with the forty wounds.

Fraternal nails of betrayal.

How can I talk to you
(I know you can hear me, though speak you can't)
the footprints of your "friends" vanished
on the silver platter with your soul
the chorus of saints
your mother hunched over the crib of the lambs.

"Be weary of the look of things
and of the antics of saltibancos".

Yet, it won't be long before
the abscess breaks open
it won't be long before
the frequent detonations of sins.

SHADOWS OF CANDLES

That's how these things are done
how come you didn't know?
Go ask the jurists
then come back
(if you so wish of course
or if the guards would so allow)
to step into the castles of philanthropy.

Couldn't the guards predict
the taper that they lit
at the centre of the square
would soon give in
to the will of the wind?

Didn't they know that nature never jokes
smile though it does at times at our whims?
How easily did they forget
the candles of the incubators
them too blown away
by the raging wind?

The lawyers of course are very well aware of
the complicated corridors
the pathways and the corners of the castle
nevertheless the roads are full
of shadows from snuffed out candles unlightable
and the darkness has filled our soul with mud
and we are piled wretched bodies
along the height of the castle.

INTO THE BACKBONE OF THE WOOD

Since the candles are flickering,
since it is up to the wills of the winds
whether the candles will for long annoy
the expanse of the darkness,

There is nothing else to do than stay awake
in front of the vigil lamp
studying the dispositions of the birds
indifferent
to the cracks of time
whence thirsty shadows emerge
asking for light and water,

Since the waggling of the living is perpetuated
around furtive twinkles
their glass luggage forever
unclaimed at ports of entry,

There is nothing else to do than carve
into the backbone of the wood
the definitive rulings
of the competent persons on duty.

Even when the soul
finds no repose
in counting its forty
gaping wounds.

NOT EVEN TWO CLOCKS

Not even two clocks
have I managed to synchronize
in so many years.
I have no knowledge of what the clocks are counting
(if there is something to count
or if they are just slicing the big moment
into lesser ones).

Nor can I predict of course
when the pointers will come to a halt
even if I detect with magnifiers and microscopes
each particle of dust
even if day and night I dust
the mechanisms of the clocks.

METALS OF REMEMBRANCE

Waking up at midnight
for the third shift at the mine.
In the old bus with the miners
breathlessness in your bag
at mountain peaks
searching for the meaning
of ceaseless wandering
of the descent into damp galleries
lit dimly by lanterns.

I never learned your craft
and now I find it difficult
to weld the metals of remembrance
if fire exceeds the appropriate limit
then on the floor pieces collapse
akin to amorphous mass.

Of course you knew the right temperatures
for welding any metal
though even then you could perceive
the impermanence of every figure
against the onslaught of rust germs
the angels of moisture.

Yet you knew
that one day the bus would sleep forever
on the mountain slopes
merciless bindweeds sprouting
out of its engine.

GYPSY WOMEN IN AGHIOS DOMETIOS

I don't remember if those gypsy women in Aghios Dometios
thoroughly read your palm;
if behind the sparks of your welding
they saw the shadows dancing
as if on Easter Day,
though bitter wine they were offered
by the survivors and their antics.

I do remember though how stubbornly
you put them to the test
making successive questions
to see how much they really knew about our clan
with every little detail.

The fright in which they later covered their eyes
against the blinding glare of your welding!

Then they'd collect their bundles and leave
even as you were welding the fragments
of desperate gestures
lying supine
under an elevated Morris Minor.

UNWITTINGLY

Like weeds sprouting between
the gears of dead engines
where formerly dazzling limousines
now rest.

How impudently they docked
outside your store
and how they lusted after the workers' cars
trudging up the hills
never quitting
in fact with stops on mountain peaks rejoicing
for being oblivious to death.

As if the limousines would never depart
for the auspicious fields
as if they wouldn't smear
with their expensive oils
the earth nobody knows
when it will yet again open its jaws wide.

Like grass carried away
with the first gust of wind
to the ends of the abyss
where souls mourn
when the petals of old
unhealed roses open up
and from the stems
tears drip down our body
with all their thorns.

EVERYTHING I NEVER DARED

I don't know what our teachers told you
but what you asked us
was blunt, distressing too.

On your workbench – pipes, hammers, tin, electrodes
tanks of acetylene and oxygen all around
the welding mask
the shining sheet metals.

(Why am I now telling you what I never dared tell?)

Neither can I learn
if now you have found the answers
you anxiously pursued
nor if where you are now
the pomegranates bloom, partridges sing
nor if you remember the bitterness of life
and supplemental joys
nor if there's something you need
nor if you can hear or see us
nor if the infectious lava
has covered our souls by now.

SEAMING MEMORY WITH ELECTRODES

I am looking in our storeroom
for your old electrodes
to weld memory's fragments.

To place them inside stainless cases
fighting rust and the elements of nature
that know not
of the passions of the soul
how acrid they make the water
as night falls.

Seaming memory with an electrode
to sustain
the moments of your life
the sorrow in your gaze...

And if pain seams the steep
slopes of the abyss together
and explosions break the universe down
and if inside the jaws of the earth
your body now lies,

In the stainless expanses
of orchards
you walk alone
looking at the edge of heavens
leaving behind the boat
where now cringes maliciously,
tentacles folded
and stinger submerged
into the infectious stream of the river,
Charon's spouse.

WITHOUT THE LIGHTS OF THE MOMENT

"Let those around you content themselves
of doing something..."

— Nikos Engonopoulos,
"A sonnet somewhat pessimistic"

Instead of becoming a maker
of fireworks and other elusive accessories
of panic and joy,

Instead of nailing smiles
into iron façades
and crosses into the spines of misdemeanours,

You chose to put on your overalls
and bend over your bench –
though never in front of the sons of men.

That's why at your burial
tears were never discharged
the minute hands never splintered

(Nor would you have liked that, of course)

That's why the clocks carried on
counting peacefully the ringing of the bell
without the lights of the moment
and the horrendous squibs.

INVISIBLE FIGURES

It was as if you were somewhere else that evening
while all of us gathered around you –
as if you saw figures invisible to us.

The next day there was nothing reminiscent
of your evening departure
though you were anxiously looking
at loose pages from your diary
putting them in order.

How can we now put in order
thousands of scattered moments
how can we rescue them
before the wind catches up with us
before the jaws of the earth catch up with us
and everything vanishes with you!

THE DUST IN YOUR LUNGS

Why should fumes and black dust
settled into your lungs
bother the caretakers?

An insignificant detail,
the dust in your lungs.
The main thing now
was to build the beams and columns
the roofs
doors and windows
systems of alarm and escape.

The dust in your lungs
was your problem and yours alone.
Couldn't you deal with it courageously for once?
And on your own!

CONCEALED TEARS

The cat was lying by your feet
and you were looking at it, calm
forgetting about the ailments lurking
in the corners of our yard like maladjusted dogs.

And yet! The cat could sense how much you suffered
and so it rubbed and rubbed again
up against your legs
looking either at you or at our mother
watering the garden.

Then it would get up and leave, hunched,
lest you should notice its tears
lest you should understand…

LIKE DRIED LEAVES

Everything was tied up with a thread
a fine thread
like dried leaves
quivering in the breeze of Spring.

We earnestly hanged up the days
to dry on the mast
then sat back by the oars
yet these swarms of uninvited birds
have no intention of leaving our boat.

And the sun sighs with us
and our days are dripping desperation.

ARE YOU BIRDS?

Our boat is filled with birds
birds on our shoulders, on our heads
perched on our hands and oars.
Under their weight we bend
and our boat groans.

What more do you want, you cursed things?
Why did you fold forever your wings?
Is it because you aren't birds
and our eyes betray us?

But if you do pulverize us
then you exist
even if sailors do not see you
from other ships
even if they say we are deranged
longing as we do to chase you away.

LAYERS OF DUST

I wasn't even born yet
when you ballyhooed your ice-cream
in the streets and neighbourhoods of Lefkosia...
Yet I remember mother
proudly showing us
the utensils for your craft.
Though now I can't recall...
Do they lie somewhere or no longer exist?

Though now I am afraid
I'll find them only
in the storehouse of memory replete with dust
layers of dust that ravage the molecules of matter
layers of dust that threaten
the marble even
supposedly playing carefree with the light.

AS IF IT HAD A SOUL

In vain have I tried to find
a photo of your first car
which you tended dearly as if it had a soul.
Indeed, it had a soul;
after all, it never betrayed you!

And also (I don't know whether it lies somewhere now
or if its engine is filled with grass and lizards)
how unwearyingly it carried
no matter how much weight we put in it
just as on that day
when we left Lefkosia in hot haste
with so many others.
How did we manage then to control ourselves
(and mainly how did it manage)
when the guards of "national salvation"
stopped us in the middle of the street
long queues of cars behind us.

I don't remember now when and how
you decided to give it up
but I do remember clearly
that afterwards many times you confessed
it would be better
not to abandon it
it would be better
to tend to it until the end.

IF YOUR SOUL

If your soul is travelling
where are its footprints?
Unless it plunges
into the distant landscapes of mist
unless it's already tired
of the bitterness of the ground
the volatility of the winds.

If your soul soars
into the depths of the sky
how does it betray
the body so cruelly?
Unless now it's taken up residence
within the idol of its body.

If your soul broke free
from the bitterness of the world
how does it let us
chase chimeras
tied to the hindquarters
of possessed horses
how does it let us smell
hazard in the air
sleep in the battle dress
wake up deranged
because of the nightmares of worldly things?

If your soul can see us
why doesn't it show us
where the secrets of life
lie hidden deep
where the solutions
to relentless math problems are kept
the answers to permanently

Trials on Welding

unanswered questions?

UNFINISHED NOTES

The stranger with the lynx's plumes
took your diary and torn it asunder
without so much as caring
about your unfinished notes.

If he cared
he wouldn't throw prayers
and icons out the window,
the wall clock
(which carried on ticking)
he wouldn't install himself on your bed
until he saw your soul
leaving through the window

The cat he didn't even notice
as it boldly climbed the vineyard trellis
and higher still
bursting into sobs
when your soul ascended into heights
the cat was unable to reach.

INCURABLE CLOCKS

"Time is a child playing at draughts,
A child's kingdom."

— Heraclitus

I wonder if the caretaker knew
looking at the wall clock all day
incessantly recording your production
I wonder if he knew
that the minute hands were deceiving the hour hands
that the second hands could no longer tolerate
the cruel slavery so they procrastinated
that the clock in general
was out of control?

Who knows if this wasn't a product
of a tacitly protesting watchmaker
of someone at any rate
who went mad listening to the furious
ticking of clocks by the hundredths?

Has anyone told your caretaker
since then
that clocks count only our illusions?
Even if he pretends not to understand,
why don't we denounce the deception unilaterally?
And the watchmakers?
At last, whose side are they on, silently bending
with their magnifiers
over the mechanisms of incurable watches?

EVEN IF IT WAS SAID BY SOCRATES

"Soul, you don't have
another shelter
in this world..."

— Argyris Chionis,
"*Ideogrammata: Tanka*", XVI

The cat wasn't worried
looking at the wall clock
nor could it save us
as we bent down to count the muffled sounds
within the jaws of the earth.

You kept asking persistently, father
but it turned its gaze elsewhere.

And while we nearly believed
that Socrates was one of us
(how skilfully he lured us
into the tentacles of dialectics)
now it seemed he was coming from somewhere else.
How did he know so explicitly
(as if he'd travelled there many times)
every corner of the Underworld?
How did he prescribe with so much certainty
the future of every soul
according to its sins?

And while we nearly believed
that Socrates was one of us
(he actually pretended not to know a thing)
there he is now, knowing everything
with such certainty

not only about our glass world
but also about the fate
of our soul and his
(especially his)
which would install itself, as he proclaimed
"bodiless ... in yet more beautiful abodes".

We listened to him in awe.
Still, your cat didn't buy it.
Even if it was said by Socrates!

UNRULY SPARKS

You wouldn't bet your life
that one day the gypsies would give an end
to their wanderings.
In fact we were jealous of them
for singing passionately at night
around their fires on the hills.
How easily they were carried away
by the unruly sparks
and travelled with them!
And how quickly they would plan
their next displacement.

You wouldn't bet your life, father,
that the gypsies were jealous of us
for burying our secrets
in chests inside our bedrooms
then drawing the curtains shut.
I wonder who we were hiding from.

Except that we didn't understand
how easily we were sometimes carried away
by the songs of the gypsies in the night
by the rebellion of sparks in the sky
and the nocturnal fleeing of balance sheets
from prudent homes
and the flamboyant dresses of our dreams
on the pillows of paroxysms
into the cases of perfume bottles.

IMMATURE WOOD

You ascended the paths
of holy waters with our mother
and the immature wood of life
would look at you and sing.
The hills ascended with you!

In terror did you see many preceding
carriages falling into the void
the horses pallid in the clouds
dripping fiery blood
onto the ground that came alive
and sought for bodies.

And when you arrived overwhelmed
at the centre of the village
they were all gone from the army camp
except for some old dogs
and famished cats.

And as you were ready to leave
cats dematerialized akin to prayers
high up the clock of the Administration Office.
And dogs akin to curses
in the empty wards of the camp
mess tins on the floor
along with bottles of iodine and gauzes.
At the background nightingales were singing.

And as you were finally leaving
some other poor cats
leaped out of the departed engines
to come to you
the venom of our generation
dripping from their tongues.

"Remember me, O Lord,
who was it that picked up the buds
of immature wood
how did the soldiers get tied up
to the hands of the stopped clock
pointing passionately
to unaccomplished reports of motion
and dried oils
onto velvet medals?"

WOUNDS

Then you started to complain frequently
that you, the master of welding techniques
the master of the most challenging metals,
was now unable to
so much as lift up
the shards of metal
from the floor and the walls of our house.

Even our mother's broom
failed to sweep them up
and my brother's magnets
admitted their first defeat.

Embarrassed we kept looking at them
now walking with great precaution.
And mother paradoxically
admitted for the first time
she could no longer tolerate
the endless orders of the cleaning supervisors
at the Bank of Credit
who knew nothing of the wounds
on the floor
and the walls
of our house.

WHITE BIRDS

How did our home become filled with birds
and how strangely they look at us
with their horrendous eyes.

They fly like demons from room to room
they creep in everywhere
even into cracks in the walls
even into gaps in the floor.

We open the windows, but nothing!
The white birds won't leave.
How persistently they wrap us up in gauzes
how they remain vigilant by our bedside of stone!

We would give anything for the birds
to finally let us
close cracks and gaps
get ready
for the attacks of insects.

THE BEES

So much hurt inside the house
and bees in our garden
wouldn't let us be.

Who would harvest the flowers?
Their eyes saw too much
but still they celebrated
even when they saw us
filling in the gaps in the floor
the gaps becoming wider still,
taking care of the walls
their cracks swelling
dangerously still?

And the bees with their honey
and the flowers with their songs
and we pensively reading
the entry "pericarditis"
taking a stealthy look at our father
leaning over our mother's bedside
and the Virgin at the edge of her bed
with a hair wreath
made of flowers from our garden
and the bees like prayers
on every tearful flower
that yielded bitter honey.

HOLLOW WALNUTS

"But all was false and hollow..."

— John Milton,
"*Paradise Lost*", Book 2:112

Suddenly the house was full of
myriads of flying ants.
How they lifted and whirled us
around the lamps
as if we were feathers!

(It was the first time you grinned, mother,
at the nightshift nurses
and father slightly smiled next to you
and fortunately neither of you knew).

And while the ants were sometimes dunking us
into the abyss of the floor
and other times wedging us between the Symplegades
of the gaps in the walls
there arrived Catalano
who changed appearances and manners all the time.

First he asked for the blessing of the Virgin.
How did he hide in the abyss
to re-ascend into the light
and start painting the walls
with heavy words and blasphemies
without so much as ask us?

No sooner did you return home,
than with a leap he sank into the earth again
only to reappear before us

incensing
and chanting
and the Virgin could no longer stand him.

And Catalano used woodchips
to fill gaps in the floor
and wounds in the walls
as the flying ants were fiercely
taking us out the windows.
Then incensing and chanting he resumed!
And so the Virgin had had enough of him
and dumped him.
And no more costumes
and masks did he have
in his suitcase
to keep on hiding,
Catalano the despicable.

EVERYTHING'S SETTLED

Everything's settled as required.

Your memoirs sealed
the letters you didn't have time to read
have now been archived
the phone calls you never answered
have now been answered
necessary explanations given.

Everything's settled as required.
Employees at their offices
the unemployed with their allowances
the poets in their cells
the dead in their beds
the sparks in their cases
the living in their illusions.

Our debts have been paid
the checks are cleared
our prayers offered
our oblations reciprocated
silence consolidated
as a token of essential respect
and designated mourning groans are prohibited
tears have been subjected
to microbiological analysis
the poets were declared in absentia
and brought to trial
generally everything has been settled
as it should be
exceptionally and graciously.

Even our souls have been folded
like clean bed sheets

devotedly deposited
in carved wooden chests to melt
with mothballs running out
without the microbes of grief
without the onslaughts of insects.

Everything has finally been properly settled!

THE SECRET TEARS OF YOUR SOUL

> "I don't know what it is, I can't cry.
> I don't understand it. [...] Help me Willy,
> I can't cry. It seems to me that you're just on
> another trip. I keep expecting you."
>
> — Arthur Miller, *"Death of a salesman"*

Wait for me, Linda. Never stop waiting for me.
What would I do with your tears now
or with the other manifestations of mourning?
You should know, Linda, that the soul of Willy Loman
is headed only to your soul
not to the sky or the Underworld.
You should know that the soul of the salesman
will forever vanish
on the day you shall stop looking for it
the day when you finally realize
I' m not away on a trip just for a while.

Why are you asking me to forgive you, Linda?
What should I do with the tears
and the staginess of funerals?
Only for the secrets of your soul do I thirst
and inexhaustible tears
only for those do I yearn
only with those do I want you to cool the rocks
of my wounded soul.
Remember that, Linda.
Prepare a warm corner in your soul
for me to plant my seeds at night
to make plans for life like a teenager
and have you summon me to bed

to which I will reply it's still early
and I am not sleepy.

REVERENT CHESTS

Souls are not asking us for blood
milk and honey
barren heifers or sheep
chasing their chimeras.

They are only thirsty for our tears
but not for those theatrical and vain ones
that move the crowds
the other ones those hidden
in reverent chests
we rarely open
and not to everyone.

Then the souls come alive
and you can hold
the soul of your father in your arms.

And if you hear weird voices at night
it's the souls asking for your unfading tears
not those theatrical ones
the other ones those hidden
in the carved wooden chest of your heart.

IF ONLY YOU HAD THE STRENGTH

What more should I tell you, father,
to make you come with me?
Don't you see the fiery tongues
don't you hear the clatters,
the battle cries of the Achaeans?

If only you had the strength of Aeneas!

"And then he carried him on his back
and rescued him
from the ferocious intentions of the Greeks".

If only you saw the smoke in the horizon on time
if you heard the war cries of the barbarians
if you carried your father on your back
if only you consumed his last Communion word!

SPARKS OF A BRIGHT CLOUD

"O anima che se' là giù nascosta..."

— Dante Alighieri,
"Divina Commedia: Inferno",
Canto XXVII, v.36

Despite their material composition
as a result of the friction of stones, metals and other elements
as a result of the combustion of wood, evidence
or arsons and so on
sparks (unfortunately for many)
are not for sale.

And that's why they try in vain
before a large crowd and journalists
to awake the souls with lyrical pyrotechnics
crackers, illuminations, flares, fireworks.

But the souls seek other things.

And the square empties out
(as retailers of souls wrack their brains
to understand what went wrong).

But as each one returns home
how dangerously the grindings in the corners
(and indeed without the sorceries of the merchants)
begin to redden
next to flammable memories.

And the souls mellow
and they ascend with the sparks
thronging small spaces

waiting to live out
even for a bit
what they missed in this life.

That's why every night in his lodge Laertes
converses alone with the sparks
that swirl maniacally
around the soul of Anticlea.
That's why his apprentices hear him
and say it's certain; without a doubt, the old man has gone mad!

THEY STAY HERE

They saw you were happy with the little things
and threw a fit.
How could they understand
that money rattling in their safe box
the shares and the chrysobulls
and the stolen dreams
they kept locked in their drawers
could only stay here?

They saw you and thought you didn't understand
but you did understand – very well indeed!
It hurt you though
not being able to believe
(like me, I confess)
that one day they would pay for their sins
in the cauldrons and the lakes of turbulent lava
in places seen, as said,
by enlightened saints and crowned poets.

Unless everything has been written using poetic license.

Even if they continually invoke
the voice of the Lord
or importunately claim
to faithfully follow the likeness of Virgil.

CRAFTSMEN OF RARE JEWELS

"Dilci, che 'l sai: di che sapore è l'oro?"

— Dante Alighieri,
"*Divina Commedia: Purgatorio*",
Canto XX, v.116

They said they knew the taste of gold –
the craftsmen of rare jewels.
How delicate their tools on the bench
how neurasthenic their precision scales!

But you, who fought against rust
knew what they sold was never pure
those masters of alchemy and mixtures.
And their scales could not speak…

That's why they kept on selling unperturbed
lotus flowers and promises in baskets
as craftsmen above any suspicion.

While you, who tormented humble metals with the sledgehammer,
never learned the art of beating around the bush,
of manoeuvres, of nonsense, of ramblings.

YOUR DAYS ARE NOT LEAVES

"You fall from the branch and cry? Why? Don't you know you are a leaf?"

— Argyris Chionis,
"*When silence sang and other inconsequential happenings*"

Your days that are falling
are not destined for the recycling bins.
Your days are not leaves
your thoughts are not trees
but their roots are threatening
your lungs and your heart
their leaves rot
within your cells.

Your days that are falling
know that they are falling
but you don't burn them
with all their putrid cells.
As if they would ever fertilize
your ailing trunk.

But you are not a tree
for passers-by to hung
their handkerchiefs on its branches
like banners of a victory
eagerly anticipated by the dead
yet one that never comes.

And they cry under the ground
and they wake us up at night
and they ask for their trophies

and we put them back to sleep
with hollow promises.

CLOISTERED AGIASMATI

The dead are not babies you can put to sleep
and take a rest. Even if they do dig in the yard
of the cloistering Agiasmati.

And then they dance
on lighted coals
summoning the living who long
to quench their thirst.
And you can hear them
but it's as if you are nailed to your mattress
as if you're bound hand and foot.

And they set off to go to Matins
with age-old monks
praising with the holy offspring
the glory of the Cross.

St. Mamas sings too riding his lion
the fighter of great miracles
the lamb sings too
perched in his arms
but suddenly it leaps out and runs to the iconostasis
yearning for your father's caress
(to whom once you couldn't explain
how the saint managed to tame the lion).

The tears of the lion
are dripping down the voracious floor.

And what if the dead of the Underworld wake up
and Minos commands
that souls be counted?

TREACHEROUS RIVER

"...oft-times the quiet river
undermines the wall unmarked"

— Callimachus, " *Epigrams*":44

A treacherous river almost non-existent
eats away at the rocks and the ground
in the subsoil of your memory.
Where souls lean forward
but you send them away.

Yet they come back thirsting
and, bending low,
you lean with them over the river.

Then the river is revived
and binds them to its tentacles
immersing them in its void
to keep them from hurting it declares,
and for you to remember nothing
but the moments
dripping rhythmically
down the shallow well of the present.

ROUGH INFLAMMATION

Shallow river
you dangerously infect
the estuaries of my memory
who's going to stop you
though you be shallow
for how long will I be sinking
with the icons
into your rough inflammation
who's going to bring me
forth from your ailing womb
how will he cleanse me
of your dissolvent liquids
in what manner will he remove them
from my mind and heart how will he rescue the dead
from the darkness of your river bed?

LEAVES OVER THE GRAVE

If doctors didn't reside
in their sicknesses
if the saints didn't abandon
their icons
if the judges didn't trample
on their scales
if the committees didn't move
to their remote passages
if nothing was left of lions
than their teeth
and of poets
than warped words,

then leaves wouldn't fall
with all their might
over your grave
and weeds
wouldn't sprout up so impudently
from the cracks
of our granitic will!

AND THEN NOTHING

Liquid darkness and then light
a garden of tears
blistering cries
behind the hills
cymbals, rattles
ephemeral joys
and victories
and scattering to the wind.

And then light
and then being naked
and then nothing
without so much as your name.
Thick darkness, water
rocks and bones.

Then back to the light
listening to tales
that sweeten the truth
being still, looking at your dreams
as they gallop into the light
unaware, shameless.

LAND SURVEYORS

The land is there to be possessed
said the land surveyors
to their measuring tapes.

But when, a few days later, we saw them
hugging the stones and the stars
among the rotten leaves,
only then did we realize that the land
is not there to be possessed
but to possess us
and finally swallow us up.

To imprison us in her womb
lest we should be reborn –
transgressions and maladies
and indelible stains of sins.

I'M SEARCHING FOR MY SOUL. WHERE CAN I FIND IT?

I didn't know why you welded the most sensitive metals with the solder. They are not all the same, you said, they too have sensitivities * never mind that they look alike * they too have their worries * for how long can they swallow the offences of the boors * they too have their sicknesses * not to mention that the filthy rust and that whore dampness pay no attention to them * not to mention that even God forgets about them, left in storerooms fraught with that fucking dust * son, the soil weighs me down * don't expect spectacular changes from this welding * nor any frolicking from the sparks * just a goody-goody fume * and wear your mask, don't suffer as I did * take care of your mother * even here there are queues * that's what they told us * that one day our turn will come for the second death * even here they say due respect is required * lest we make noise and perturb the order of the universe. Take care of them all, don't mind their nonsense and the insipid fairy tales. Nothing, son, nothing! So stop living my death, stop slaying your life. These rocks weigh me down * and if now I talk to you, I couldn't do it without your voice * my cells gradually disintegrated * they went back to my mother's womb * never mind that I suddenly left for the paths of Holy Waters without saying a word * deep inside I knew it * I didn't want to become a burden for you * now I'm searching for my soul * but where can I find it with all these keepers fencing us in * we should apparently wait for the designated procedures and other bullshit * apparently they failed to notice that the soil has devoured us * mind you, collect the beads of my worry beads and don't run along the rails of time like crazy * there is no point to it * let that rascal run behind you panting * and if it catches up with you * rub it in, show it bad news and circulars * so that at last it leaves you in peace. Don't worry about a thing. Just don't tangle with the river. Let it rage when it sees me watering my mother's orchard, barefoot in the matudinal hours * before sinking back into the earth's embrace. I wish I could find the vein of the holy water * even if I had to stay forever behind the bars of its embrace * not to disturb your sleep. But never mind me. I am sure I will find the vein soon * the fleeing has exhausted me and how could you then convince Mother that you couldn't stand the thirst and you escaped. She cannot understand. You're crushed by the walls of her womb and all she does is doll up in front of her mirrors, full of compassion!

Table of Contents

BY THE SAME AUTHOR	3
ALONG THE PATH OF AGIASMATA	7
THE GLARES REMAIN	8
VIGILANT SPARKS	9
DEPARTURE	10
THE COINS	11
STERILE SENTIMENTS	12
THE DUST	13
ROWING AWAY ON YOUR OWN	14
ANO MADARI	15
SHADOWS OF CANDLES	16
INTO THE BACKBONE OF THE WOOD	17
NOT EVEN TWO CLOCKS	18
METALS OF REMEMBRANCE	19
GYPSY WOMEN IN AGHIOS DOMETIOS	20
UNWITTINGLY	21
EVERYTHING I NEVER DARED	22
SEAMING MEMORY WITH ELECTRODES	23
WITHOUT THE LIGHTS OF THE MOMENT	24
INVISIBLE FIGURES	25
THE DUST IN YOUR LUNGS	26
CONCEALED TEARS	27
LIKE DRIED LEAVES	28
ARE YOU BIRDS?	29
LAYERS OF DUST	30

AS IF IT HAD A SOUL	31
IF YOUR SOUL	32
UNFINISHED NOTES	34
INCURABLE CLOCKS	35
EVEN IF IT WAS SAID BY SOCRATES	36
UNRULY SPARKS	38
IMMATURE WOOD	39
WOUNDS	41
WHITE BIRDS	42
THE BEES	43
HOLLOW WALNUTS	44
EVERYTHING'S SETTLED	46
THE SECRET TEARS OF YOUR SOUL	48
REVERENT CHESTS	50
IF ONLY YOU HAD THE STRENGTH	51
SPARKS OF A BRIGHT CLOUD	52
THEY STAY HERE	54
CRAFTSMEN OF RARE JEWELS	55
YOUR DAYS ARE NOT LEAVES	56
CLOISTERED AGIASMATI	58
TREACHEROUS RIVER	59
ROUGH INFLAMMATION	60
LEAVES OVER THE GRAVE	61
AND THEN NOTHING	62
LAND SURVEYORS	63
I'M SEARCHING FOR MY SOUL. WHERE CAN I FIND IT?	64

TRIALS ON WELDING WAS PRINTED
BY Ἐπὶ Σχεδίας PUBLICATIONS
& LEONIDAS GALAZIS
IN NICOSIA 2015.

www.ingramcontent.com/pod-product-compliance
Lightning Source LLC
Chambersburg PA
CBHW071413040426
42444CB00009B/2224